The Transliteration of Modern Russian
for English-Language Publications

The Transliteration of Modern Russian
for English-Language Publications

J. Thomas Shaw

THE UNIVERSITY OF WISCONSIN PRESS

Madison, Milwaukee, and London, 1967

Published by the University of Wisconsin Press
Madison, Milwaukee, and London

U.S.A.: Box 1379, Madison, Wisconsin 53701
U.K.: 26–28 Hallam Street, London, W.1

Printed in the United States of America
by Waverly Press, Inc., Baltimore, Maryland

Library of Congress Catalog Card Number 66–22858

PREFACE

Whenever Russian names or other Russian words appear in a publication not printed in Cyrillic, some system or systems of transliteration must be utilized. That there can be no totally satisfactory, all-purpose system of transliteration of the Cyrillic alphabet into any non-Cyrillic alphabet is well known; and for different kinds of readers different accommodations need to be made. To the English-speaking reader who is not familiar with the Russian language, a transliteration system should suggest something about the pronunciation of that language; the less the reader knows of Russian, the closer the transliteration needs to be to something representing fairly accurately the pronunciation of the words. But transliteration, in any publication, should be *transliteration* rather than an attempt to catch pronunciation when it varies markedly from the Cyrillic spelling (e.g., the ending *-ogo*, though pronounced as though it were *-ovo* in English, should be transliterated according to the Russian spelling).

The four systems of transliteration presented in this manual range from one usable in works intended for the general reading public to those suitable for the needs of specialists in various fields. These systems are designed to handle the problems encountered in transliterating modern Russian Cyrillic; it is assumed that authors will follow the generally accepted practice of transliterating Old Style Russian (used in Russia until 1918) as though it were New Style. (See p. 9.) The special problems of transliterating Old Style Russian Cyrillic for library cataloguing and for linguistic discussions in linguistics works fall outside the scope of this manual.

J. Thomas Shaw

Madison, Wisconsin
June, 1966

CONTENTS

Preface   v

Four Systems of Transliteration and
Recommendations for Their Use   3

Transliteration Chart   8

Special Problems and Suggested Solutions   12

A Note on Russian Dating   15

The Transliteration of Modern Russian
for English-Language Publications

Four Systems of Transliteration and Recommendations for Their Use

System I

System I is acceptable for transliterating *personal and place names*, both in such publications as newspapers and popular magazines and in books directed to any audience whose interest is not primarily in Russian studies. System I is appropriate for names occurring in translations of literary works to be published separately or in popular magazines or journals. It may also be used in scholarly studies in the natural sciences, in the social sciences, or in Russian literature, when the audience sought is not composed solely of specialists in Russian studies in that field.

For example, a popular journal or newspaper article on travel conditions in Russia would use System I for names of people and places; so would a scholarly study of a literature other than Russian in which incidental references were made to Russian writers or a general history of World War II in which Russian personal and place names were mentioned.

System I is *not* satisfactory for transliterating words as words

3

or citations of bibliographical material. See the discussions of Systems II and III for suggestions on handling words as words and bibliographical citations in publications in which System I is used for personal and place names.

System II

System II, the Library of Congress system for transliteration of modern Russian with the diacritical marks omitted, is recommended for use by those scholars in the social and natural sciences who are concerned with Russian studies. In publications of works in these fields, System II should be used for *all citations of bibliographical material*, and it may be used for *words as words*. Whether it is used for personal and place names in the text proper (in non-bibliographical matter) will depend on the extent to which the work is directed to specialists.

For example, a professional journal for specialists in Russian studies in the social sciences or in a particular field of social science may appropriately use System II throughout; similarly, other works (including dissertations) directed exclusively to such an audience may use System II consistently.

If System I is used in the text proper for works in the social or natural sciences when they are aimed at an audience broader than one of specialists, System II should be employed for transliteration of words as words and for documentation in all citations of bibliographical material. Thus System I may appropriately be used for personal and place names in the text in a general work on European history which includes a discussion of Russian history, in a general professional journal in history, and in a special study of a particular problem in Russian history for an audience which does not consist solely of specialists in this field; in each case, words as words and all citations of bibliographical material should be transliterated according to System II.

System II is not, in general, recommended for use in bibliographies published as separate volumes, but it may, for practical reasons, be used for such works as computer-set publications of library holdings.

System III

System III is the international scholarly system for the transliteration of Russian, used by linguists and literary scholars specializing in Russian and Slavic studies. In publications directed primarily or exclusively to linguists or literary scholars, System III should be used for *words as words* and for *all citations of bibliographical material*. Whether it is used for personal and place names in the text proper (in non-bibliographical matter) may depend on whether the publication is directed particularly to Russian (and Slavic) scholars.

For example, in a professional journal devoted to Russian (and Slavic) linguistics and literature, and in other works (including dissertations) addressed directly to specialists in these fields, it is appropriate to use System III consistently throughout. On the other hand, an article on Turgenev, for example, in a professional literary journal not limited to Russian or Slavic literature may use System I for personal and place names in text, but words as words and all citations of bibliographical material should be transliterated according to System III. For an annotated English-language edition of the letters of Pasternak, it would be appropriate to use System I for the text proper, and System III for transliteration of words as words and in all citations of bibliographical material.

System III is the most acceptable one to use for bibliographies in literary or linguistic publications (for example, the "Annual Bibliography" in *PMLA*) and for separately published bibliographies if the audience is to be an international one (for example, *The American Bibliography of Slavic and East European Studies*).

System IV

System IV is the Library of Congress system of transliterating modern Russian with diacritical marks. For *separate bibliographical publications*, especially in the social sciences, this system is satisfactory. If the audience is an international one, however, System III is usually preferable for bibliographies in book form.

Mixtures of Systems

As suggested above, the nature of a publication and the audience for which it is intended will determine which transliteration system is appropriate for the text proper of any particular work. For example, System II has been recommended for use throughout dissertations on Russian subjects in the social sciences and System III throughout dissertations on Russian (or Slavic) literature or linguistics. For subsequent publication of such dissertations in book form, however, System I might be used for names in the text proper, if the audience toward which the work is directed is no longer composed solely of specialists in this field of Russian studies. System II or III—as appropriate to the field of study—would, nonetheless, still be used for all citations of bibliographical material and for transliteration of words as words.

In any type of publication not directed primarily to Russian specialists, System I may be used for the transliteration of personal and place names. Even in such works, however, System II or System III, as appropriate, should be consistently used for words as words and for all citations of bibliographical material. In any case, a single system should be used for transliterating personal and place names within the text proper of a publication, and a single system (which may or may not be the same one) for *all* information—including personal names, place names, and the titles of the Russian works—in the citation of bibliographical material. (See "Special Problems," pp. 12ff., for the exceptions to this rule.)

In any one publication, no more than two systems should be used. If System IV is used at all in a publication, it should be used throughout.

Transliteration Chart

Transliteration Chart

	I	II	III	IV		I	II	III	IV
А а	a	a	a	a	Р р	r	r	r	r
Б б	b	b	b	b	С с	s	s	s	s
В в	v	v	v	v	Т т	t	t	t	t
Г г	g	g	g	g	У у	u	u	u	u
Д д	d	d	d	d	Ф ф	f[4]	f[4]	f[4]	f[4]
Е е	e[1]	e	e	e	Х х	kh[5]	kh[5]	x[6]	kh
Ё ё[2]	yo	e	e	e	Ц ц	ts	ts	c	t͡s
Ж ж	zh	zh	ž	zh	Ч ч	ch[7]	ch[7]	č	ch
З з	z	z	z	z	Ш ш	sh[8]	sh	š	sh
И и	i	i	i	i	Щ щ	shch[8]	shch	šč	shch
Й й	y[3]	i[3]	j[3]	ĭ	Ъ ъ	—[9]	''[10]	''[10]	''[10]
К к	k	k	k	k	Ы ы	y	y	y	y
Л л	l	l	l	l	Ь ь	—[9]	'[11]	'[11]	'[11]
М м	m	m	m	m	Э э	e	e	è	ė
Н н	n	n	n	n	Ю ю	yu[12]	iu	ju	i͡u
О о	o	o	o	o	Я я	ya[13]	ia	ja	i͡a
П п	p	p	p	p					

8

Combinations of Letters

	I	II	III	IV
-ый (in names)	-y[14]	-yi	-yj	-yĭ
-ий (in names)	-y[15]	-ii	-ij	-iĭ
-ия	-ia	-iia	-ija	-iia͡
-ье	-ie	-'e	-'e	-'e
-ьи	-yi	-'i	-'i	-'i
кс	x	ks	ks	ks

Other Letters of the Old Style Alphabet

The letters shown below, in use in Old Style Russian, should, for general purposes, be transliterated as though they were the corresponding New Style letters. (Note: In transliterating Old Style Russian, one must be mindful of the changes of spelling of certain grammatical forms [especially genitive adjective case endings] and pronouns, and transliterate them as though they were spelled in New Style.)

Old Style	New Style
I i	И и
Ѣ ѣ	Е е
V ѵ	И и
Ѳ ѳ	Ф ф
Ъ ъ (terminal)	omitted

Notes on Transliteration Chart

1.   In System I, the spelling *ye-* may be used initially (e.g., Yevtushenko). It should *not* be used intervocalically (Alexeev, *not* Alexeyev; Dostoevsky, *not* Dostoyevsky).

2.   This symbol is not considered a separate letter of the Russian alphabet, but a pronunciation variant of *e*. The rules for its use are very complex. In System I, where pronunciation is emphasized, it should be transliterated as *yo* (e.g., in such names as Alyosha, Lyova, in fiction); in Systems II, III, and IV, it should ordinarily be transliterated as *e*, but, if it is important to distinguish this symbol from *e*, it may be transliterated as *ë*. Usage within a single publication must be consistent.

3.   See also Combinations of Letters.

4.   Not *ph* (e.g., Epifany, *not* Epiphany).

5.   The transliterations *h* and *ch* for this letter should be avoided.

6.   The transliterations *ch* and *kh* are *not* acceptable for transliteration of this letter into English in this system.

7.   The transliterations *tch* and *tsch* for this letter should be avoided.

8.   The transliteration *sch* for this letter should be avoided.

9.   Simply omitted, with no indication of omission.

10.   The symbol " is used to transliterate the Russian letter ъ (the hard sign). The symbol " for the hard sign is preferable to the symbol " (used for double quotation marks), and, when copy is marked for a printer, this symbol should be distinguished from quotation marks. When a word containing this symbol is set in italic, the symbol should also be set in italic and will look like a double prime mark: *"* .

11.   The symbol ' is used to transliterate the Russian letter ь (the soft sign). The symbol ' for the soft sign is preferable to the symbol ' (used for the single quotation mark and the apostrophe), and, when copy is marked for a printer, this symbol should be distinguished from a quotation mark. When a word containing this symbol is set in italic, the symbol should also be set in italic and will look like a single prime mark: '.

12.   The transliteration *iu* for this letter should be avoided in this system.

13.   The transliteration *ia* for this letter should be avoided in this system.

14.   Preferred, instead of *-i* (e.g., Bely).

15.   Preferred, instead of *-i*, for both prenames and surnames (e.g., Dmitry, *not* Dmitri; Dostoevsky, *not* Dostoevski).

Special Problems and Suggested Solutions

Place Names

It has been recommended that a single system of transliteration be used for all place names and personal names within the text of a publication, and a single system (which may or may not be the same one) for information—including place names—in all citations of bibliographical material. (See "Mixtures of Systems," p. 6.) Within English text, however, place names with Anglicized spelling in widely accepted usage may follow that spelling: e.g., Moscow (for Moskva), St. Petersburg (for Sankt-Peterburg or S.-Peterburg). For citation of the place of publication of Russian works, the following abbreviations may be used: M. for Moscow (Moskva), L. for Leningrad, SPb. for St. Petersburg (Sankt-Peterburg, S.-Peterburg).

Russians with Names of Non-Russian Origin

Non-Russian names of Russians should be transliterated as though the names were of Russian origin (e.g., Dal or Dal', Benkendorf, Vulf or Vul'f, Fet, Fonvizin). Names of authors of non-Russian origin who made their reputations writing in Russian should be treated as though they were Russians (Gogol or Gogol', Bulgarin, Senkovsky).

Prenames

Prenames of Russians should be transliterated according to the appropriate system, rather than put in the form of English equivalents: e.g., Ivan *not* John; Vasily or Vasilii or Vasilij, *not* Basil. *Exception:* Russian rulers' names should be printed in the conventional English form if the patronymic is not furnished: e.g., Michael I, *but* Mikhail Pavlovich (or Mixail Pavlovič). Names which closely approximate English names (e.g., Aleksandr for Alexander; Petr for Peter) may be printed in the English form in System I, but they should be directly transliterated in Systems II, III, and IV.

Surnames of Russian Women

When the Russian form of a woman's surname is different from the masculine form of the same name (e.g., Pushkin's wife was Pushkina, Dostoevsky's was Dostoevskaya), the treatment in English will depend upon the audience, the number of such women's names, and particularly on whether the text uses the names without prename. In Systems II, III, and IV, the feminine forms should ordinarily be used; in System I it will depend upon the considerations cited above.

Thus, in System III, Puškin's wife is Mme Puškina, or Natal'ja Nikolaevna Puškina, or N. N. Puškina. In System I, Pushkin's wife is Mme Pushkina (or Pushkin), or Natalia Nikolaevna Pushkina (or Pushkin). Although, in Russian, initials are often given instead of first names for women, this practice should be avoided when System I is used. In dealing with the names of Russian women, when a feminine form is given prominence (as in a book title), it must be remembered that it *is* a feminine form: thus, if the ridiculous is to be avoided, the surname of Anna Karenina's husband must be given as Karenin, and the problem of consistency in handling the names of all the women in the work must be kept in mind.

Russian Wives of Non-Russians

The prenames should be transliterated from Russian, using the appropriate system; the surnames should be given their Latin-alphabet spelling.

Names of Individual Russians
Who Have Accepted a Western Spelling

In general, these surnames should be spelled in the Latin-alphabet spelling which the individual himself accepted, e.g., Mirsky, Herzen. In bibliographical material of Cyrillic publications, the precise transliteration should be used.

Surnames with Differing Common Western Spellings

Publications directed primarily to Russian specialists should as a matter of course consistently use direct transliteration under the appropriate system for all surnames of Russians, even though other spellings may be common in English. In such publications, the name of the revolutionary Chaykovsky (or Chaikovskii) and that of the composer would be spelled the same way: the spelling Tchaikovsky (French transliteration) or Tschaikowsky (German transliteration) would not be used. It is to be hoped that directly transliterated spellings may eventually supplant for English-language publications the forms which have been adopted from other languages.

Clerical Names Based on Latin

These names should be transliterated following the appropriate system, rather than going back to Latin spelling (e.g., Foty, *not* Fotius; Epifany, *not* Epifanius *or* Epiphanius).

Anglicized Words

In general, such words should be given a spelling acceptable to a standard American dictionary: kolkhoz, ruble, sovkhoz, boyar, droshky, Bolshevik, Soviet, calash. When alternative English spellings are given in such a dictionary, the one most closely approximating direct transliteration is preferable. For example, the forms kopek, tsar, tsaritsa, and Tatar are preferable to the alternatives kopeck, czar, czarina, and Tartar.

Bibliographical References to Materials Published in Non-Cyrillic Languages

Such references should use the spellings found in the actual publication (e.g., *The Letters of Chekhov*, as the title of the English-language publication).

Old Russian Orthography

Old Russian orthography should be transliterated as though it were new orthography, except for citations in historical linguistic investigations and for library cataloguing, which involve considerations too complex to be treated here.

A Note on Russian Dating

The Julian (Old Style) Calendar was used in Russia until 1918. To convert Old Style dates to New Style (according to the Gregorian Calendar), add 10 days in the years between 1582 and 1700, 11 days during the eighteenth century, 12 days during the nineteenth, and 13 days during the twentieth. In the Soviet Union, February 14, 1918 (New Style), followed January 31, 1918 (Old Style).

In Russia, the system of dating "from the creation of the world" was used until the beginning of the eighteenth century. The creation of the world was thought of as having taken place on March 21, 5509 B.C. To change dates "from the creation of the world" to our system, subtract 5508.

The first day of March was considered the first day of the year in Russia until about 1492; and after that, September 1, until the year 1700, when January 1 was decreed the first day of the year.